DOMINANCE:
FACT OR FICTION?

Barry Eaton

"Learning is best done by challenging the old mythologies and this book surely does that".

Prof Ray Coppinger

CONTENTS

Wolves Wolves Wolves Wolves . . . . . .

ACKNOWLEDGEMENTS

My thanks to:

Prof Ray Coppinger for allowing me to use his photographs, for his invaluable advice and for sharing with me some of his immense knowledge – and for keeping me thinking!

Dr Ian Dunbar BSc, BVetMed, MRCVS, CPDT for his encouragement, words of wisdom and for his contribution to the book.

Robert Falconer-Taylor BvetMed, MRCVS, Dip CABT, and Peter Neville BSc (Hons) for their invaluable contribution

The Centre of Applied Pet Ethology (www.coape.org) who started me questioning the concept of 'dominance'

Monty Sloan of the Wolf Park, Lafayette, Indiana for the use of some of his wonderful photographs of a wolf (www.wolfphotography.com)

Mrs Sylvie Derrick and Tarn for raising such a wonderful litter of Border collies

To Jay Lorenz and CC Guard for the use of their photographs

My wife, Carol, who had to read, re-read and read again the manuscript and continually corrected my grammar

And to my old dog Jess who missed her vocation as being a canine super-model!

FOREWORD

Dominance: Fact or Fiction is a little book with a big message. Without wasting words, Barry Eaton dispels the dominance myth and its insidious rank-reduction programme, which is nothing more than an arduous task for owners to make their poor dogs' lives a misery. "Give them a scalpel and they would dissect a kiss."

The dominance myth "logic" flow chart is flimsy at the best but scary at the worst. The notion is that:

1. Wolf social structure is entirely explained by a linear dominance hierarchy in which there is a constant battle to be alpha dog and dominate the rest of the pack.

2. Domestic dogs are descended from wolves and so the same must apply to them.

3. Domestic dogs are trying to dominate us.

4. We should issue a pre-emptive strike and dominate dogs by enforcing strict rules harshly.

In actual fact:

1. Wolf social structure is a wee bit more involved and sophisticated that a single linear hierarchy – this is merely a Mickey Mouse interpretation. Wolves have special friendships and allegiances and by and large, wolves live together harmoniously.

2. Dogs are very (VERY) different from wolves. Domestic dogs were selectively bred for thousands of years to be less fearful and more easily socialized to people. If wolves and dogs were the same, many people would be sharing their homes with wolves.

3. Oh! Get a life!

4. This has to be the flimsiest, most thinly-veiled excuse for little-brained, *schadenfreude* types to label poor dogs as our adversaries in the training arena and in the home.

Why on earth do we treat our best friend like our worse enemy? How on earth can anybody think that a dog is trying to dominate his owners by eating first, going through doorways first, enjoying the comfort of furniture, playing games of tug-of-war, eagerly pulling on leash, or relieving himself in the house? Dogs are not politicians. Dogs are not masters of subtlety or innuendo. Dogs are straightforward and they live in the here and now. If a dog wanted to dominate his owner, he would do just that. End of story. Even so, when dogs bark, growl, snap, lunge, nip, or bite, rather than being aggressive or dominant, the dog is usually, understandably, simply fearful of domineering owners

The "thinking" behind the dominance myth and the Spartan, boot camp, rank-reduction programme is silly to the point of hilarious. Sadly, downright silly thinking becomes extremely serious when dogs are neglected and mistreated as a result. Indeed, many unsuspecting dog owners are bullied by misguided trainers to abuse their dogs under the guise of "training."

Certainly, rules are important – any rules – for example sit means sit, and shush means shush. Usually, the owner knows best, especially when the dog's safety is concerned. Also, when dogs and people live together, either we can live with dogs in their doggy dens and adhere to their rules, or dogs can live with us, in our homes and abide by our rules. It is just so much easier for people to teach dogs our household rules and regulations. Moreover, because each dog/human relationship is quite unique, each owner should decide on *her* household rules for the dog. Each owner should decide where the dog sleeps, for example – on the bed, in the bed, on the bedroom floor, downstairs, on the living room sofa, in a dog bed on the kitchen floor, outside, or in a dog kennel. It is up to each owner to make decisions for her dog. As long as the owner can instruct the dog to lie in his kennel, or to get off the bed, then it's no problem – the dog may sleep wherever the owner wishes.

The greatest joy of living with a dog is being part of creating the most unique inter-specific relationship, wherein "two are halves of one." Enjoy this book. Enjoy your dog.

Dr Ian Dunbar *PhD, Bsc, BVetMed, MRCVS, CPDT*

1. INTRODUCTION

If you only take one fact away after reading this book, I would like it to be the fact that a dog is a dog and not a wolf in dog's clothing.

Over the past 30-40 years, when pet dog training started to become popular, virtually every dog training class based their training methods on the need to dominate the dog, part of which included using 'pack rules'. We were told we had to treat our tame, domesticated dog as a wolf; a wild animal, and this was perpetuated by the number of dog training books popular at the time. Even today, books and videos based on this method are still published and, in my view, cause confusion amongst pet dog owners in encouraging them to ensure their 'dominance' over their pet dogs by being alpha in their family pack.

The premise of pack rules is that the dog descends from the wolf resulting in the following misleading conclusions:

- As the dog descends from the wolf, a dog's behaviour will be that of a wolf.

- As grey wolves form packs with a structural hierarchy, dogs will also form packs with a structural hierarchy.

- As the domestic dog lives with humans, he is part of our pack and we have to treat him as a pack member.

Nobody stopped to question this line of thinking until recently. Over the last few years, authorities in dog and wolf behaviour have started to question the relevance of treating our dog as though he was a wolf. Many books have now been written (some of which I refer to in the following pages) that dispel the myth that our dog, given the chance, will try to raise his status over humans. Current knowledge and thinking are questioning whether we are right to compare our dog's behaviour to that of its distant cousin, the wolf.

The purpose of this book is to pull together as an overview, many of the arguments that have been put forward by eminent authorities on dogs and wolves as to why our dog is **not** a wolf and therefore should not be treated as such, and provide an alternative view to 'dominance'.

I believe it's time to open our minds and consider the concept of pack rules a thing of the past and recognise that dogs' are not plotting to dominate their owners.

2. FROM WOLF TO DOG

Training methods 30 to 40 years ago were based on dominating our dog, with all the harsh, punitive methods that it involved. The reasoning for this type of training, we were told, was that as the dog descended from the wolf, he still retained a wolf's mindset. In other words he still thought as a wolf and we should treat him as a wolf in dog's clothing. Sadly this type of training still goes on even today by trainers who have not moved with the times. Some trainers still hand out a list of pack rules to people attending their classes that impose a totally unnecessary strict regime on their dog. The concept of dominating a dog because he descended from the wolf regardless of how distantly related they now are has become so ingrained into our training methods, that we have lost sight of any other possible way of training our dog. But not any more.

Pryor (2002) says, *"Dominance hierarchies and dominance disputes and testing are fundamental characteristics of all social groups from flocks of geese to human governments. But perhaps only we humans use punishment to gain for ourselves the reward of being dominant"*. She goes on to say that if you want a dog to change his behaviour, *"it's a training problem and you need to be aware of the weaknesses of punishment as a training device."*

Donaldson (1996), says, *"The whole dominance idea is so out of proportion that entire schools of training are based on the premise that if you can just exert adequate dominance over the dog, everything else falls into place. This is dangerous."* and she goes on to say it means *"that incredible amounts of abuse are going to be perpetrated against any given dog"*.

The good news is that more and more dog trainers are using positive, motivational training methods such as food, toys, and clicker training to reward a dog for getting something right. These training methods do not rely on 'dominating' the dog; they are more about creating a symbiotic relationship between owner and dog where the learning experience is fun for both, resulting in a better trained, happier dog.

Yet why do some people still believe the dog has a hidden agenda and that he wants to be 'dominant' over his owner or raise his status over members of his human family? Do some dogs *really* want to raise their status within a human 'pack'? Do we *really* have to be 'dominant' or 'pack leader' over our dogs? Do the 'pack rules' we have long been told to apply to our dogs actually work? Does a dog *understand* what we are trying to do when we apply pack rules? Does a dog *really* think he is part of our 'pack', as many dog training books tell us, or simply part of our 'social unit'?

Ah, questions, questions. But ones that need asking - and need answering!

Could it be we are fixated on the idea of the dog being part of our 'pack' because of the popular misconception that as wolves form packs so domestic dogs form packs? Humans live in a culture of hierarchies. From cradle to grave, whatever walk of life, we are almost always answerable to someone. It might seem natural then, to pass this hierarchical mindset onto our relationship with our dogs and believe that as dogs 'instinctively' form packs, they would perceive themselves as being part of our 'pack'. Therefore they must have their place within it and to meet with our own hierarchical structure, their place should be at the bottom.

Are we living under the misconception that a dog is a 'natural' pack animal? We have two species of animal, human and canine, living together as a social group. However, it has long been the belief that dogs and humans together form one pack and in that pack the humans must be dominant or alpha over their dogs. I believe there is a flaw in this reasoning.

In order to understand why domestic dog behaviour is not the same as wolf behaviour, we must understand at least a little about how a wolf pack is structured and how it works. Generally, a stable wolf pack consists of a mated pair and their immediate offspring. This is known as a 'nuclear family'. However pack dynamics are not necessarily straight forward as packs could also consist of an 'extended family' which includes siblings and their offspring; a 'disrupted family' where one or both of the parents are missing; or a 'step-family' which has accepted a wolf from another pack (Packard 2003). So pack structure and dynamics are not necessarily straight forward, but the point is that these packs are best viewed as families, and are

4

usually made up largely of related, co-operative animals. Many wolves at the age of about two or three years will leave the pack and go in search of a mate to start their own pack. These wolves are known as 'dispersers'. Rather than stay in the 'nuclear family' where there is little chance of mating and passing on their genes, these lone wolves will risk the elements of the wild to search for another lone wolf of the opposite sex.

The grey wolf form packs in order to survive and produce offspring. They have to adapt to their environment, in many cases they need to kill large prey to feed offspring and all members of the pack. This can only be done with a number of wolves forming a pack, even if the pack consists of only the two parents, and cubs need to adapt to pack behaviour at a very early age if they are to survive. Can it be then that forming a pack is not genetic but more a strategy for survival? Prof. Ray Coppinger has studied both dogs and wolves for many years and says about packing behaviour, (2001), *"Research indicates that packing behaviour is a developmental response to a particular habitat....Wolves don't always pack; some populations never pack."* And of dogs, he says, *"I don't see much in dogs that indicate they have the fundamental behaviours that would allow true wolf-like packing."* The question as to whether packing is not a genetic behaviour is supported by a hypothesis by Schmidt and Mech (2000), *"We believe wolves live in packs primarily because adult pairs can then efficiently share with their offspring the surplus food resulting from the pair's predation on large prey"*. Therefore if wolves don't instinctively (genetically) form packs, why would dogs? More importantly, wolves form packs with their own species, so why would a dog form a pack with a different species, humans for example?

If a domestic pup is not socialised with other dogs during the critical socialisation period, he may well become fearful of other dogs and may remain so, possibly for the rest of his life. Several dogs living together in one household will learn to live together in contentment providing they have been socialised with dogs at the right age and in the right way. According to Dr Ian Dunbar (1979), *"In the majority of instances, pack formation in domestic dogs would seem to be an exception rather than the rule"* He goes on, *"The notion of hierarchies has been much overplayed. For the most part, dogs seem to live in relative harmony with each member of the **group** (my* emphasis), *each generally going about its business with an apparent disinterest in the affairs of others"*

If, in the majority of cases, dogs can live quite happily together in a social group, why would they feel the need to be part of our 'pack'? In reality, our domestic dog has no reason to form a pack with his human owner as every need for his survival is provided for – by us. And if the dog has no reason to form a 'pack' with us, there is no reason why we should 'dominate' our dog or be alpha.

When is a Wolf not a Wolf? When it's a Dog

Before putting forward what will hopefully debunk pack rules, I think it's important to understand why a dog is not a wolf. According to the Taxonomy by Clutton-Brock (1999), there are 38 species classified in the Canidae family. It includes the wolf (*Canis lupus*), Figure 1, where we believe it all started.

Fig. 1
Canis lupus
Courtesy Monty Sloan, Wolf Park,
Lafayette, Indiana.

Fig. 2 *'Honey', a domestic dog*
(Canis familiaris) chewing her bed!

And it includes the dog *(Canis familiaris)*, Figure 2, which is where we're at today.

Despite many hypotheses over several hundred years as to which of the Canidae family is the dog's ancestor, science indicates that the dog *(Canis familiaris)* is descended from the wolf *(Canis lupus)*. The reasons for this conclusion have been well documented

6

in many publications and are not really the subject of this book, but the primary reasons we believe the dog descended from the wolf include;

- The mitochondrial DNA is virtually the same between them
- They have the same number of chromosomes (78)
- They have the same number of teeth (42).

During the course of evolution there have also been some major physical changes.

The dog's teeth became smaller, more crowded and jaws became weaker. There are now three shapes of head (Penman 1994);

- Mesaticephalic: the shape most like that of a wolf, if somewhat smaller, is a medium length muzzle typically seen in German Shepherds, Labradors, and Terriers. About 75% of all dogs have this shape head.

- Brachycephalic: a short, wide muzzle, typically seen in Pug, Pekingese, Shih Tzu, Bulldog and Boxer where the eyes are set towards the front of the skull

- Dolichocephalic: a long, narrow muzzle typically found in sight hounds where the eyes are set at the side of the skull

The skull on the left in Figure 3 is that of a 43Kg wolf. The skull on right is of a 43Kg dog. A dog's brain became about 20% to 25% smaller than the wolf's, speculating that wolves are more intelligent as they have to 'work' to survive, and the smaller brain means

Fig. 3
*The skull of a 43Kg wolf (left)
and a 43Kg dog (right)*
Courtesy Ray Coppinger

7

a dog's senses of sight and hearing being less acute than a wolf's. The brain became smaller as it needs calories to grow, so when Man started to build camps and settlements, wolves with a short flight distance remained on the village dump but consumed fewer calories. It was these wolves that over time became more domestic, tamer and ultimately became the domestic dog's ancestor. Wolves that had a long flight distance and ran away quickly if disturbed relied on killing their natural prey which has a higher calorific value and remained wild. (Coppinger 2001).

A dog bitch has two oestrous cycles a year and comes into season any time of the year starting between the ages of 6 and 12 months. Compare that to a wolf bitch that doesn't come into season until she's about two years old and has one oestrous cycle at the same time every year so her pups are born in the spring when it's warm and food is more plentiful (Kreeger, Packard 2003). A male wolf may not become fertile until 22 months of age and then will only be fertile during the mating season (Kreeger 2003), that is once a year. A domestic dog, at reaching about 6 months of age, remains fertile every day of his life.

Results of domestication have affected the dogs' ability to communicate through facial and body language. They don't fully mature and remain in a developmental stage resembling that of a juvenile wolf throughout their life. (Lindsay 2000)

Over several thousand years, dogs of many breeds and types we know and love today have evolved from the wolf. While the wolf itself may have changed little over this time, we have produced, through a combination of nature and nurture, dogs of all shapes and sizes. The size of a domestic dog can range from a 680gm Chihuahua to a 95kg St Bernard. The wolf has stayed within the same size range and the coat colours haven't changed over thousands of years.

We have dogs with different gaits, tail carriage and ear shapes than a wolf. We have bred dogs to help man, for guarding, retrieving, herding, pulling sledges, hunting, assistance dogs for people with disabilities, and dogs to sniff out drugs, bombs, and a plethora of other substances, or just lapdogs. A dog's coat can vary in colour, length, and type and we even have breeds with no coat at all. For example, the Komondor has a naturally long white coat of matted hair; a Labrador Retriever can be sand coloured, black or brown. A Chinese Crested has a little patch of coat on his head, tail and paws but there is no coat on the remainder of his body so he needs sun block to stop him getting sun burnt in summer and man-made coats to keep warm in winter. A Newfoundland has been used for water activities over so many years that they now have webbing between their toes. A few generations ago, Golden Retrievers used to be a 'Golden' brown, but now many are a light, sand colour. In some instances we have bred the same breeds for the show ring and as a working dog. One is bred for looks and conformation to meet a breed standard set down by Man; the other is bred for his working abilities. We therefore breed for looks and we breed for behaviours.

We have even changed the dogs' gait. At some point during their running action, sight hounds will have all four paws off the ground, which is in common with the cat family! Wolves will always have two paws on the ground when running.

Wolves rarely bark and when they do it is very subdued. Some dogs bark all the time! In fact during evolution, we produced breeds that tend to bark more than other breeds, the Spitz breeds for example. We also have breeds that bark very little, like the Shiba Inu and Basenji

The dog's brain has changed. It no longer thinks like a wolf because it isn't a wolf. Primarily, a wolf concentrates on three things; 1) hazard avoidance, so it doesn't get injured and die; 2) hunting, so it can feed; and 3) reproduction, so it can pass on its genes. A dog has different values to the wolf. A dog's values are what he finds rewarding within his environment. Things like food, toys, walks, companionship, playing with his owner, doing agility, fly-ball, retrieving, herding, and all the other things we have introduced into our dog's existence.

The frequency of a wolf's innate motivated behaviours (motor patterns) differs from a dog's. For example, they have to learn fear response quicker than a dog, 19 days for a wolf opposed to 49 days for a dog. Wolves have to learn very quickly to hunt and kill in order to survive. Generally, a domestic dog doesn't have to learn hunting and killing skills.

A wolf's predatory motor pattern has never changed over many thousands of years. It is still;

Orient > eye-stalk > chase > grab-bite > kill-bite > dissect > eat

During evolution of domestic dogs, some parts of the sequence of the predatory motor pattern have been enhanced while others have been deleted or made latent. (Coppinger 2001)

A Border collie's predatory motor pattern for example is:

Orient > **eye-stalk** > **chase** > dissect > consume

Fig. 4 *A characteristic 'eye-stalk'*
part of a Border collie's motor patter.
Courtesy Ray Coppinger

Fig. 5 *The Border collie 'chase'.*
Courtesy Ray Coppinger

In a Border collie's motor pattern, the 'eye-stalk' and 'chase' (see Figures 4 and 5) are the most rewarding parts of the sequence. You'll notice 'grab-bite' and 'kill-bite' are missing, but although those motor patterns are still there, for the most part, they are latent. Unfortunately when I was participating in sheepdog trials the 'grab-bite' was not altogether latent in my dog. There were a few trials where I was disqualified when my dog over enthusiastically grabbed a hind leg of a sheep, but we also won some trials as well!

A Retriever needs to retrieve game with such a 'soft mouth' (see Figure 6) so as not to bruise it, so a Retriever's motor pattern is;

orient > chase>**grab-bite**>consume

10

Fig. 6
A Labrador Retriever 'grab-bite'.
Courtesy Mrs CC Guard

The change in predatory motor patterns is further demonstrated by Dr Erik Zimen (1983). Zimen kept a pack of wolves and a pack of Standard Poodles in adjoining pens and observed their different behaviours. In one experiment he gave a chicken to one of the wolves and a chicken to one of the Poodles. His observation of the wolf and chicken was that the wolf quickly devoured the chicken, while the poodle just pulled out feathers and didn't eat the chicken.

On one hand, we have a wolf whose predatory motor patterns have never changed because they need them intact in order to survive. On the other hand we have our domestic dogs of different breeds or breed types with totally different motor patterns that have adapted to suit the breed of dog whether as a pet/companion dog or as a working dog.

Steven Lindsay (2000) says about the differences in behaviour between the wolf and the domestic dog; "*A long history of domestication behaviourally segregates dogs from wolves, and one must take care not to overly generalise between the two canids in terms of their respective motivations and behaviour patterns.*"

We still have the wolf (*Canis lupus*) that has remained unchanged for centuries, and we have the domestic dog *(Canis familiaris)* that has changed in looks and behaviours and can now do many things that are totally alien to the wolf. Dogs are now as far removed from their ancestors as we are from ours.

3. DOMINANCE – WHAT IS IT?

We are now up to date and the wolf has evolved into the domestic dog and herein lays the problem! When dog training and behaviour counselling in particular, became fashionable and more widespread during the 1980s' and 90s', many books were written about how to raise a dog using pack rules and to treat behavioural problems by using pack rules as a rank reduction programme.

Behaviourists and trainers alike jumped on this bandwagon. It was generally assumed in many cases that any behavioural problem was due to the dog being 'dominant' by trying to raise his status within his human 'pack'. Therefore the diagnosis was based on wolf-like behaviour. If the dog was trying to raise his status, the remedy was based on what wolves would do to resolve the problem. So we humans had to mimic wolf behaviour to lower the dog's status.

This raises two issues:

1) what do we **think** we mean by the word 'DOMINANCE', and

2) where did the pack rules come from? (And that's not such a silly question!).

The Concepts of 'Dominance'

The human definition of Dominance: According to the Concise Oxford Dictionary, 'dominant' is defined as *"Having commanding influence over.... be the most influential or conspicuous.... holding commanding position over."* If however, we apply this definition to our dogs, we would be applying human values to our dog's way of thinking. One might argue that an aggressive dog can be fairly conspicuous and influential, which I wouldn't necessarily disagree with. But the dog has not made a conscious decision to be conspicuous and influential in the same way a person may consciously decide to become conspicuous and influential.

A dog trainer taking a class will probably stand in the middle of a hall, talk to their clients and demonstrate how to teach their dogs to do something. The instructor has consciously decided by the fact s/he wants to run training classes, to be conspicuous and influential and to hold a commanding position over their clients; it goes with the territory. Some people strive for high office, to have more people work for them and to take on more responsibility. This is a conscious decision to be influential and to hold a commanding position over other people. Conversely some people are shy or reserved and would not dream of standing up and talking to a hall full of people. They have made a conscious decision *not* to be conspicuous and influential. We therefore have a **choice** to be conspicuous and influential, whereas a dog cannot consciously make that choice. Therefore the human definition of 'dominance' would not apply to our dogs.

The wolf concept of dominance: According to Danish ethologist Roger Abrantes (1997), 'dominance' in wolves is *"a drive directed towards the elimination of competition for a mate."* In other words if a wolf wants to breed and pass on his genes, he must eliminate the threat from other wolves to become alpha. This doesn't mean he goes around beating up other male wolves, as Abrantes goes on to say, *"The hierarchy is defined as a dominance-submissive relationship established and maintained by means of ritualised behaviour."*

Being alpha is having the right to produce off-spring. Given that we control most, if not all of our dog's resources including whether s/he can breed or not, the wolf's concept of dominance, the *"drive towards the elimination of competition for a mate"*, wouldn't apply to our dog.

Fig. 7
Wolves performing 'ritualised behaviour'
Courtesy Monty Sloan, Wolf Park, Lafayette, Indiana

In Figure 7, the wolf on the right is the alpha male; the muzzle at the back is that of the alpha female. The other two wolves are their offspring. This is a 'meet and greet' situation using *ritualised behaviour*, which is genetic canine behaviour.

If we really felt it necessary to be alpha over our dog, how could we establish and maintain by means of *"ritualised behaviour"* in canine language so the dog would understand? The answer is - we can't. We don't have the same ears as a wolf; we don't have a tail. We can't raise our hackles; we can't show a similar set of teeth or curl our lips in the same way as a wolf. We can't dilate our pupils in the same way. In short, we are not equipped with the same anatomy as a wolf or a dog to be able to communicate in a way that a dog (or wolf) will fully understand. In short, we cannot mimic canine *"ritualised behaviour"*.

Resources: Many behaviour counsellors and forward-thinking authorities on dogs hypothesise that dominance in our domestic dogs is about access to, or control of, resources which could result in resource guarding. Resource guarding is where a dog has something it prizes and may show aggressive behaviour to hang on to it at all cost. Neither dominance aggression nor access or control of resources has anything to do with status. From our point of view, if we want to call a dog 'dominant' then we should look no further than who controls the resources. This appears to be a more logical concept than 'dominance equals status' when we consider what a dog's values are; food, water, shelter, somewhere to sleep, playing with toys and many other things depending on the dog and his environment. It all boils down to resources.

Dr Karen Overall (1997) says, *"Dominance is a concept found in traditional ethology that pertains to an individual's ability to maintain or regulate access to some resources. It is not to be confused with status".*

Overall is not alone in her views. To support her hypothesis of dominance equating to resources, Overall cites Hinde (1970) as saying *'Dominance may not be synonymous with hierarchical standing. Dominance has been traditionally defined as the individual's ability to maintain or regulate access to some resource'*

In the 1970s' biologist Geoff Parker developed a theoretical model called Resource Holding Potential (RHP) that is still used by scientists today. RHP is a mathematical equation that predicts the likelihood of an animal engaging in conflict with another, usually of the same species, in order to gain or retain a resource. The generality of the model is that it applies to all species of animals, including humans. The model assumes that animals do not enter a potentially physically harmful conflict situation before each has assessed (or 'sized up') the other in terms of ability to 'win' and the value of the desired resource over which the conflict has arisen. It is to the advantage of each individual to have an idea in advance of the likelihood of their winning or losing. The RHP model predicts that a few losses carry more 'weight' in terms of deciding what to do in similar conflicts in the future as does winning. You can see this happening in dogs that have become 'trained losers' – in even the most friendly play encounters with other dogs in the park, they roll over on their backs in appeasement and even urinate. On the other hand, dogs that have learned that using threats of aggression works in getting, or keeping what they want may develop an expectation of winning conflicts over resources. Clearly, this has absolutely nothing to do with status and everything to do with the resources the dog values most and the strategies he has developed *through learning* to hang on to them.

Dominance Aggression

Many people believe that if a dog is showing aggression to his owner he is being dominant and thus, trying to raise his status. Not so. Entire chapters in dog books have been written about 'dominance aggression' so I will try to summarise what it means. Overall (1997) has a discrete definition of dominance aggression as *"Intensification of any aggressive response from the dog with any passive or active correction or interruption of the dog's behaviour or access to the behaviour."* This means simply, that if a dog is suffering anxiety due to the behaviour of people towards him, he may become aggressive.

However, as 'dominance aggression' is based on some form of anxiety problem, Dr. Overall has redefined the term as 'impulse control aggression'. Dogs are not impulsively aggressive if they are of good breeding, have been socialised correctly and have not been mistreated. But we know some dogs can be pushy. They test the boundaries to see what they can get away with. Dr. Overall stated at the US Association of Pet Dog Trainers Conference in Orlando, (2003) *"there is no evidence that these pushy dogs are anything other than a variant of a normal dog, and there is no association with any kind of artificial rank hierarchy......and there is no evidence that pushy dogs develop any form of pathological aggression."*

To support Overall's view, Lindsay (2000) states, *"Many aggressive displays that are currently diagnosed as dominance aggression are aimed at avoiding some perceived aversive outcome rather than establishing or maintaining the offending dog's social status."*

Alexandra Semyonova (2006) has studied a group of dogs through their natural lifetime and in their natural environment. In her resultant paper she says says, *"In many case, the inflexibility of human behaviour leads to interactions involving aggression. In first instance, the human is the attacker."*

A dog may become aggressive when an owner can't read the dog's body language, in particular the dog's non-threatening signals. The dog is trying to convey something, but the owner misunderstands and takes inappropriate or no action, or gives mixed signals that only serve to confuse the dog. The dog may respond aggressively if being mistreated or being harshly corrected. He may be uncertain of the relationship with his owner or with people generally, and possibly react aggressively if something happens that he perceives as a threat. Or he may be suffering from another form of anxiety that the owner hasn't recognised. This then is a dog reacting, albeit inappropriately from our point of view, to a situation he is not totally happy with – but it has *nothing* to do with status.

The Dog in Our Family

When pack rules for our dogs were introduced, there was an obsessive belief that if we didn't treat our dog as part of our pack and teach him that he was the lowest of the low, he may take advantage and raise his status. We were told that almost any problem behaviour, whether it was something we found annoying or anything to do with aggression, was an attempt by the dog to gain a higher status.

The first question we must ask ourselves is, does the dog perceive itself to be part of a 'pack' with his human family? There's no doubting that dogs are social animals and if socialised correctly and at the correct age, are able to live amicably with groups of many different species. But can a dog be part of a human 'pack'? During the critical period of social development, the interaction with siblings and dam results in imprinting of the puppy's brain. In other words, it will know it's a dog, will recognise another dog and behave accordingly. This will shape the development of the dog's future behaviour. We accept dogs into our human family but the dog cannot be part of a pack with humans because of the interaction and imprinting the puppy received in its first few weeks of life. It doesn't think like us, or behave like us, or smell like us, or live by the same values as us.

Except under certain, extreme, circumstances, packs tend to be conspecific. John Fisher (1997) wrote, *"I really don't believe that dogs look on us as other dogs and therefore do not compete with us for status."* If we accept the premise that a dog does not perceive himself as part of our human 'pack' we have to question why he would want to try to raise his status in a hierarchy over humans.

If however we really do think of our dog as a wolf in dog's clothing, then consider Abrantes's definition of a wolf trying to gain alpha status; *"a dominance-submission relationship established and maintained by means of ritualised behaviour."* Does that **really** sound like a possible relationship that could happen between dog and owner; two different species? I don't think so, but it does sound like a relationship between two of the same species.

A final point to consider; as our dogs are provided with food, water, shelter, mental and physical stimulation, company, and their health is looked after, there would be no reason for them to want to raise their status. A dog will form strong social attachment to his owner and family and vice-versa, but as part of a social group, and he will not strive to raise his status.

Origins Of The Pack Rules

Before we look at the common notion of 'pack rules' and how they are supposed to affect our relationship with our domestic dog, I think it's worth considering where they originated from and why some people have become too focused on the idea that our dogs want to be 'dominant' and raise their status over us.

Pack Rules are believed to have originated from observing a captive pack of wolves and then making a direct comparison between the behaviour of captive wolves and the behaviour of domestic dogs. They are based on the social, hierarchical structure of a captive wolf pack. In other words, if this is what a captive wolf would do, then that's what a dog will do.

However, the behaviour between a captive wolf pack and a naturally free wolf pack are somewhat different. In a naturally free pack the alpha male and female, now known as 'breeders', would breed and rear their offspring and usually initiate hunting expeditions. When there are cubs to feed, the breeding female and pups are reliant on the other pack members to provide food. At some stage in their life wolves will leave their nuclear family to find a mate in order to start their own pack, therefore alleviating any social tension. According to David Mech (1999), a world authority on the behaviour of free roaming wolves, *"in a natural wolf pack, dominance is not manifested as a pecking order and seems to have less significance than the results of studies of captive packs had implied. In a natural wolf pack, the dominance rules bear no resemblance to those of the pecking order, that of similar individuals competing for rank."* So in a free wolf pack, 'alpha' does not necessarily have the same connotation as it does in a captive pack. He goes on, *"dominance contests between other wolves are rare, if they exist at all."* Therefore there would be no 'top dog' lording over the rest of the pack. He also says, *"The typical wolf pack should be viewed as a family with the adult parents guiding the activities of the group and sharing group leadership in a division of labor..."* Females would look after the pups while the males would forage and hunt. If the kill were big enough all pack members, regardless of rank would feed together. *"If the kill were small, the breeders would eat first but if food were scarce, the pups would be fed first.*

18

If the kill were big enough all pack members, regardless of rank feed together."

Contrary to the family values of a naturally free pack, wolves in a captive pack make frequent challenges to gain higher status. The higher the position at stake the more vigorously is the campaign conducted. A captive pack will have unacquainted wolves of different ages and gender brought together from different sources. In this situation a certain amount of social tension is likely to exist, particularly during the mating season. Under these circumstances there would be a dominant male and female, and probably frequent fights from younger wolves for higher status. If the captive pack is truly 'captive' in that it is managed and manipulated by man, the wolves will be unable to express many of their natural behaviours and will be unable to leave the pack to find a mate as free wolves do.

In January 2006, the Royal Zoological Society of Scotland decided to euthanase six captive Mackenzie River wolves, a sub-species of the North America wolf. According to a press statement from the Highland Wildlife Park, *"the pack has not been portraying their natural behaviour imperative for this species. This lack of strong pack dynamics has meant that the animals have not worked together as a social unit."*

The free pack then is at risk from predators (Man, wolves and bears for example) and injury or even death by large prey. They don't know where their next meal is coming from, but they live in a natural environment in comparative harmony. A captive pack lives in an artificial, yet safe environment. They have no threat from predators or injury from large prey but there is a certain amount of social tension, and there's no opportunity for wolves to leave the pack. Therefore the behaviour between the two types of pack is quite different.

Can it be then, as there were very few free wild packs to study, the pack rules applied to our dogs have come from observations of a captive wolf pack with its ever changing social structure? If, and it's a big IF, we wanted to compare our own dogs behaviour with its distant cousin, surely we should be looking at the behaviour of a naturally free pack, rather than the adapted behaviour of a captive pack. So have we been barking up the wrong tree all these years?

But hang on a minute; we could be talking about a double-whammy. Not only have we been comparing dog behaviour to that of a captive pack instead of a free pack, perhaps we should have been asking whether making a *direct* comparison between dog behaviour and wolf behaviour was the right thing to do. From Darwin to Coppinger, there have been several theories about how dogs evolved from wolves, the consensus being that the most likely hypothesis is one of self selection; that is, the less fearful wolves became more isolated from the wild population and became more a part of a human community. Over the generations the wolves became more domesticated; later more tame; and later, trainable. Eventually, Man started breeding for particular behaviours and looks. Clutton-Brock (1999) states *"In time, these tamed wolves would have become less and less like their wild forebears because inherently variable characters, such as coat colour, carriage of ears and tail, overall size and proportion of limbs would be altered by the combined effects of artificial and natural selection. In this way, the wolf became a dog"*.

We need to appreciate that although there are many behaviours that are shared between wolf and dog, (digging, circling before laying down etc) there are also many behaviours that are totally different, which is why I believe we should not compare our dog's behaviour with a wolf's behaviour because, quite simply, a dog is not a wolf. As Coppinger (2001) says, *"A new species evolves through the gradual shifting, over time, of gene frequency within a population."* A dog is now very different to a wolf.

Now someone is going to say that their domestic dog is in a similar situation to that of a captive wolf. Like the captive wolf, a dog cannot pack his bags and leave. Like a captive wolf, a dog is managed and manipulated by Man. Even though a wolf may be in a captive pack, he is still a wild animal. Release him into the big, wide world and he will still have all his survival instincts intact. He'll still have his predatory motor pattern to be able to hunt, kill, dissect and consume prey; that is he'll still have the *orient > eye-stalk > chase > grab-bite > kill-bite > dissect > eat*, motor pattern intact. So what about our domestic dog that has ventured into the big, wide world? Well, how many stray dogs are picked up and eventually find their way into a re-homing centre looking more like a skeleton than a dog? They don't have the necessary predatory motor patterns to survive day after day without the help of humans in some way or other. Domestic dogs, generally, are not equipped to survive in the wild.

Coppinger's research has shown that feral dogs do not need to form a pack in order to survive. If all the vital elements of survival are available, food, water, and shelter, they are happy to live independently or harmoniously in small groups. Figure 8 shows a feral dog in a village in India. The dog doesn't belong to anyone and is not a threat to anyone, but his survival is still dependant on Man. The dog lives in and around the village so he can scavenge for food discarded by the human occupants and both water and shelter are available. Feral dogs have no need to hunt and probably couldn't (apart from small prey such as rodents and rabbits) due to the lack of predatory motor patterns, but all life sustaining resources are available. So we arrive back at *resources*. Doesn't that ring a bell?

Fig. 8
Feral Dog
Courtesy Ray Coppinger

4. THE PACK RULES

Back in the 1980s, and early '90s, we were almost brainwashed into believing that any sign of a behavioural problem meant our dog was being 'dominant' and was trying to raise his status over his human owners. Any training book of the day told us that we as the owner, needed to be the alpha of the 'pack' to prevent our dog becoming dominant, or in other words, trying to raise his status. Even today there are still books published and videos produced that make a direct comparison between wolf and domestic dog behaviour and suggest lowering a dog's 'status' by mimicking wolf pack behaviour.

Depending on which book you've read or what you've been told, pack rules are numerous and varied and the list of 'rules' is inconsistent. Many dog training classes still give out a list of 'pack rules' and they may vary depending on what the instructor has read or learned.

The list of 'rules' I have are:

- Eat something before feeding the dog.

- Stand in your dog's bed to show him you are alpha

- Do not allow the dog on the furniture (bed, chair, sofa).

- Don't let the dog lay at the top of the stairs.

- Don't let the dog lay in the hallway or in doorways.

- Never step over the dog.

- Never let your dog through a doorway first.

- Dogs that pull on the lead are 'dominant'.

- Never let your dog initiate the beginning or end of games or attention.

- Never let your dog win games of tug.

- Put your dog in a 'down' position

We were even advised to physically put our dog into a submissive position by putting him into an alpha roll; (that is putting the dog on its back, pressing him down while shouting at him). Zoologist, Dr Patricia McConnell (2002) says of alpha rolls, *"Well-socialised, healthy dogs don't pin other dogs to the ground. Submissive individuals initiate that posture themselves. The posture is a display signal from one animal to another, a signal of appeasement, not a wrestling manoeuvre. Forcing dogs into "submission" and screaming in their face is a great way to elicit defensive aggression. Within their social framework, you're acting like a lunatic."* It is the submissive dog that **voluntarily** roles on his back while being investigated by a higher ranking dog, so forcefully putting a dog in an alpha roll may be perceived more as an act of aggression by their owner.

Wolves display the same behaviour when one wolf 'stands over' another. Harrington and Asa (2003) say about submissive behaviour in wolves, *"Passive submission is often a reaction to approach and investigation by a dominant animal. The submissive animal lies partly on its back, with its tail curved between its legs and its ears flat and directed backwards."* At no point is a wolf or dog **forced** into an alpha roll in order to submit so why are we told to do it to our dogs?

What about us?

It's all well and good discussing how wolves behave and comparing it to our dog's behaviour but where do we mere humans fit in? Well, according to the 'pack rules', we fit in right alongside the dog together as one pack. Do you not think there is something a bit strange about that? The 'rules' are based on canine-to-canine behaviour and communication, but how can we become involved with the way dogs communicate? We cannot imitate what a dog does because we are not dogs yet the 'rules' say this is how we are supposed to behave.

Let's consider some of the rules we have been told to apply in bringing up our dogs, bearing in mind that they are based, supposedly, on how wolves behave and not how dogs behave.

Eat something before feeding your dog

This 'rule' is based on the misconception that the alpha wolf eats first. This so-called 'rule' is totally misleading. Alpha wolves **do not** necessarily eat first. Mech (2000) refers to breeders eating first if the prey were small, but if food were scarce pups would eat first. If the prey were large enough all the pack, regardless of rank would eat together.

Mech (2003) also observed 13 wolves feeding together, side-by-side, on a freshly killed moose. Only two members of the pack weren't feeding and that was because there was no room. Kirsty Peake has been observing wolf behaviour at Yellowstone Park, US, since 1999 and lectures on wolf behaviour and ecology. In a personal communication (2008) she says that a wolf moved through a resting pack with a piece of meat in its mouth. It squeezed in between two other wolves without any reaction to the presence of food from the other wolves. It's also worth noting that it is not always the alpha that makes the kill, or is even present at the time of the kill, so he won't always be the one to eat first.

A wolf bitch has invested 50% of her genes in her puppies. Her priority is to ensure their survival and she will go without food herself if necessary. Therefore it's not so much a question of 'dominance' or being 'alpha', it's more of a question of resources and survival of the young and therefore, survival of the species.

Eating something before your dog to show you are supposedly alpha is a 'rule' that does not apply to wolves, so why are we inflicting it on our dogs? And what will the dog actually learn from it? Well, nothing. Imagine it's time to feed the pup. There's dad with 12-week-old pup's food ready in a bowl placed on top of the kitchen worktop. He calls mum in from the garden where she's cutting the grass (I'm all for equality!); teenage daughter who is drying her hair while listening to the latest CDs' and teenage son who is in the garage stripping down his motorbike. They all gather in the kitchen and eat a biscuit. When they've finished the biscuit, they all go back about their business while pup eats his meal. Bearing in mind, that young pups have four meals a day this scenario will need to happen four times a day! Also what is pup going to think when the kids are at school and the bread-

24

winner is at work earning the daily crust? Is this not going to send mixed messages to the pup? Sometimes all the 'pack' is present and sometimes it isn't. What has he really learned from that? Probably that we humans are all mad!

Training domestic dogs these days is now, thankfully, moving away from 'dominating the dog' methods and is moving on to positive, motivating methods like the use of a clicker or the lure and reward method. Both of these methods use food as rewards for the dog getting something right. We now have a situation where an instructor and the owner have a bag full of treats for the dog. During the course of the training period, the dog may get to eat all the treats and the owner and instructor eat nothing. Are we making our dog 'dominant' because we are giving him all the food treats and we don't eat anything? Of course not, so why should we have to eat something at home before feeding the dog?

Overall (2003) says *"Most training books tell people to feed their dogs after themselves to reinforce the leadership status of the humans. This is wrong."*

Stand in your dog's bed

The alpha wolf is supposed to be able to sleep where he likes and will make another wolf move if he fancies his sleeping place, so we are supposed to stand in the dog's bed to show that we are alpha.

In reality, for the first few weeks, wolf cubs cuddle up together but from about 4 weeks of age they develop 'social distance' and from thereon sleep apart, including alpha. *'Contact between sleeping animals is rare and occurs mostly by chance'* Zimen (1981). Also Mech (2003) says about wolves sleeping arrangements, *"If allowed to choose their own resting sites they usually select separate ones."* So if you think your dog is 'alpha', he wouldn't be sleeping with you! In a personal communication, Peake (2008) says that over the many years she has been observing wolves, she has never seen an alpha move another wolf just to gain its sleeping place. Her colleague at Yellowstone Park says, *"All the times I've watched them* (wolves) *there doesn't appear to be any indecision or bickering over bedding spots."*

Looking at the scenario realistically, we stand in the dog's bed, we then get out and the dog gets in. What is the point? What is the dog going to learn from that? To exert our authority over our dog, the pack rule says if the dog tries to get in the bed while we are standing in it, we are told to take the bed away and make him sleep on the floor. Not all homes have fitted carpets. Some have a polished wooden floor and others may have a stone floor in the kitchen where the dog would possibly sleep. While these features may be aesthetically and architecturally appealing and enhances the character of the house, they don't make very comfortable sleeping surfaces. To deny a dog comfort and warmth is tantamount to cruelty. And just as a thought, what if the dog's bed is a crate? Or maybe you have a small dog that likes to make his bed in unusual places (see Figure 9)!

Fig. 9
An unusual sleeping place – and
a cute photo!

Fig. 10
A litter of domestic puppies eating
first – just as wild wolf pups will do.

Do not allow the dog on the furniture.

By letting our dog share our bed, chair or sofa, we are supposedly elevating him to the same status as us. If we allow our dog on the furniture at will, what we might be doing is creating a resource guarding problem which has nothing to do with status.

The dog may perceive the owner's bed, chair or sofa as a comfortable place to sleep and if he's allowed access to these resources he may start to guard them if access is suddenly denied. Some owners like their dog to be with

Fig. 11
*My dog Jess, who is showing all the signs of **not** being 'dominant'.*

them on the sofa or the bed, but to prevent any potential resource guarding problems, train the dog to come up by invitation and to get down when told.

Don't let the dog lay at the top of the stairs.

It would appear from this rule that the alpha wolf's physical position should be one that is higher than the rest of the pack. It may be so alpha can watch over the pack, but wolf pack sizes vary and can be as small as mum, dad and offspring with the family unit staying close together except while hunting. With large wolf packs, they don't always stay in the same place; they go off in family or social groups. With a pack with several adult wolves they all lay on higher ground as it's the best position to detect intruders (Mech 2003). As all or at least most of the adult wolves occupy the higher ground, not just alpha, this cannot be anything to do with status. So it would appear alpha wolf is quite happy to be on the same level as other pack members so that will also question the validity of the 'do not let your dog on the furniture' rule.

Dogs have their favourite resting places around the house where they are just content to watch what's going on, chill out or have a nap. A few years ago I had a dog that loved sleeping at the top of the stairs. It was one of her favourite sleeping places because at a certain time of day the sun would shine through a window onto the landing, on the exact spot she was sleeping. Was she being dominant? Nah! Was she being smart? You bet!

Don't let the dog lay in the hallway or in doorways.

This is because the alpha can see the comings and goings of his 'pack' we are told. As I mentioned above, a large pack doesn't always stay together all of the time so it doesn't matter where alpha positions himself, he won't be able see the comings and goings of his pack. However, if the alpha positions himself strategically, this would have more to do with spotting intruders; wolves from another pack, bears and so on, or looking after his mate and cubs.

If a dog positioned himself in the hallway it may be a resting place; in a doorway he may be keeping an eye on the owner. If this were considered a problem, it would probably be one of over-attachment and nothing to do with status.

Never step over the dog.

The alpha, supposedly, would make another wolf move. As has already been explained by Abrantes, a dominance-submission relationship is *"established and maintained by means of ritualised behaviour."* With an established social structure, a subordinate will voluntarily move when a higher-ranking wolf enters the 'social space' of the subordinate (Abrantes 1997, Mech 2003). The social structure has already been established so if moving out of the way of a more dominant wolf maintains the social structure, then so be it, but it is not a behaviour that exerts dominance. Also if alpha doesn't move a wolf when it's asleep as we've already seen, then why would he move another wolf when it's awake?

If my dog has found a patch of sunlight which means she's laying in the middle of the room, I'm quite happy to walk around her but in doing so, I'm not giving off signals of subservience to her and I doubt very much that she perceives that I am. Occasionally, I may need her to move in which case I say "excuse me" because I'm polite and that's what I've trained her to respond to. So she moves but I'm not exerting 'dominance' over her. When I ask her to do something and she responds, it's because she's been *trained* and for no other reason.

One of the requirements of Assistance Dogs International member organisations was to teach dogs to lie still while people stepped over them. The standard was changed a few years ago to remove this part of the assessment, not because it was a dominance or status issue, but because they feared the dog might sustain injury in public if it stayed lying down when someone stepped over it. Canine Partners continue to train their assistance dogs to lie still but also train the dog to 'move' when asked to do so (Bondarenko, 2007, personal communication).

Making a dog move won't make it more subservient or enforce the owner's 'dominance'. There could be good reasons for wanting the dog to move or to lie still but this is achieved by training, resulting in a well-trained dog, not a subservient one.

Never let your dogs through a doorway first.

This we are told is because it's the alpha's privilege to go first. This rule has clearly come from observations of a captive wolf pack where alpha may well go through small openings first; when transferring from one pen to another for example. But our dogs are descended from free roaming packs and in their environment, from forests to icy arctic tundra it is unlikely that there are any small openings which wolves might file into.

Even *if* owners follow this flawed rule, subservient wolves will show signs of deference as alpha goes first. People cannot mimic the posturing of an alpha (breeding) wolf, and a dog won't show a submissive posture as the owner goes though a door first, so the entire exercise is pointless. It means nothing to the dog and the owner achieves nothing.

When it's pouring with rain and the dog has to go outside to eliminate, would you go out the back door first and get soaking wet just to enforce your alpha position? I certainly wouldn't. My dogs will have to go out on their own and get wet. But by doing that, I won't be telling them that they are of a higher status than me because I can't give the right canine signals. And what would happen if you were sitting watching television with your dog lying by your side, and then he gets up and starts wandering towards an open doorway? Would you have to get up and dash to the door to make sure you go through first? And what if you have more than one dog and they're in different parts of the house? There are so many permutations of different scenarios, that to enforce this 'rule' becomes impossible – and unnecessary.

The one occasion I do agree with an owner going through the doorway first is when taking the dog for a walk. The last thing you would want is your dog pulling you through the front doorway in his excitement to get to the park, but this is just good manners and safety based on training, not showing who is being 'dominant'.

Dogs that pull on the lead are 'dominant'.

The reasoning behind this 'rule' is based on the misconception that alpha leads the way and dictates where the pack goes. The alpha may decide on the route to take but does not always lead from the front. According to Mech (2000), leading a pack can be influenced by *"youthful exuberance and oestrus"* He says, *"Wolves often follow river beds, game trails, and old roads. When doing so, it is obvious where the pack is headed for certain stretches, so any wolf may forge ahead temporarily."*

Mech also describes how he observed a pack of wolves crossing a frozen river led by the alpha. Most of the pack started to cross while some wolves were hesitant and stayed on the river bank. Part way across other wolves felt uncertain and turned back. Eventually the rest of the pack turned back. The pack therefore did not follow the alpha but instead made a co-operative decision as to which way to go.

Contrary to the reasoning behind this 'rule', the alpha wolf does not always lead first, so to say our dog is pulling on the lead because he's 'dominant' is totally misleading. Dogs pull on the lead because they haven't been trained not to, not because they are seeking a higher status. If we did follow this misguided rule, surely we should be teaching our dog to walk behind us as we are 'alpha' and the dog is subservient. In my opinion, this rule like all the others is a convenient way to explain to owners why they are having problems with their dog. Let's blame the wolf! A realistic scenario is a dog being walked to the park, and in his excitement he pulls on the lead in the hope of getting there quicker. On the way home when the dog is tired he walks nicely on a loose lead. In the meantime, the dog has been running free often ahead of the owner. But that does not mean the dog is being 'dominant' on the way to the park and while running in the park but is being subservient on the way home. I don't think that's very likely. Is the penny dropping? Can you see how flawed the pack rules are?

Never let your dog initiate the beginning or end of games and attention

As a pack rule, we have been told that the alpha wolf initiates the start of games and determines when they finish which is why we shouldn't let our dog initiate the start or end of games and attention. What we know about a free roaming pack of wolves is that adult wolves of both sexes care for and show tolerance within the family. A wolf pack needs strong social bonds. According to Mech (2003) *'The psychological tendency to form (strong) bonds results from a mere desire for physical contact. As pups grow older, physical contact continues during play and eventually occurs daily among all members of the pack.'* Also, *"any highly motivated wolf can affect the activity of its pack mates, such as play."* So it doesn't appear that a pack of wolves sit around all day waiting for the alpha to begin a game. Zimen (1981) says, *"No member decides alone when an activity is to begin or end"*

The bond between domestic dog and owner must also be strong if they are to co-habit harmoniously so why can't a dog come up for a game or attention? Dogs are social animals and need social contact. Some dogs, however, will take advantage of being given too much attention and will start to *demand* it. If owners are inconsistent in whether they give attention or not, it may result in a confused dog developing unwanted behaviours such as barking or jumping up in order to get the attention it desires. To avoid confusing the dog, owners must be consistent in their actions and train the dog. Dogs need to learn good manners and like everything else, this comes through training. It has nothing to do with status or pack rules.

Do not play games of tug

This rule refers to wolves tugging on a piece of meat and the higher status wolf would win, which is only true if the prey were small. However if food is plentiful the rule is flawed as wolves open and dissect the tougher parts of a carcass by grabbing an end of some part of the prey's anatomy and tugging against each other to tear the skin apart or to pull muscle meat from bones. Each wolf will eat whatever he ends up with. This erroneous link to wolf behaviour is misinterpreted in that a dog, if allowed to win a game of tug, would perceive itself as stronger than its owner and could lead to dominance problems.

Research into the differences between dog-dog play and dog-human play at Southampton University (Rooney, Bradshaw, Robinson, 2000) found that dog-dog play was more of a contest. Dogs behave differently when playing with other dogs than they do when playing with humans as dog-dog play is more competitive than dog-human play. No evidence could be found that dog-human play was anything more than a game, not a contest. The research concludes that *'Decreased competitiveness may mean that the outcome of dog–human games is less likely to affect the players' relationship than has been suggested by some authors.'*

To avoid any possible problem of resource guarding of the toy, train the dog to 'leave' or 'drop'. Play is important for learning, influencing behaviour and forming a bond between dog and owner. Tugging is a natural behaviour and we have enhanced that behaviour to serve man. For example, an assistance dog will tug the washing from the washing machine but it doesn't make it 'dominant'. There is nothing wrong with playing tug with a dog and even letting him win sometimes, providing you have taught the dog some etiquette like responding to the 'drop' command.

Put your dog in a 'down' position

Supposedly the lower the wolf's physical position, the more subordinate he is, so we have to get our dog in a 'down' position to show him he's subordinate to us.

I recently watched a commercial video of a dog trainer instructing a class over a six week period. All the pack rules were mentioned including the importance of getting the dog in a 'down/stay' position. The owners were told to teach their dog a 30 minute 'down/stay' just to show their dog that they are subordinate to the owner. What a miserable life those dogs must have. The owners were just pet dog owners yet they had to teach their dog a 30 minute 'down/stay'. In competitive obedience at championship level, dogs are only expected to do a 10 minute 'down/stay' but these poor dogs were expected to do a 30 minute 'down/stay', just so the owners can show their 'dominance' over their dog.

Figure 12 shows my dog, Jess. I have just asked her to lay down, and she has, so I say "good girl" because I've asked her to do something and she obeyed, and I give myself a pat on the back for being such a good dog trainer! But does she look submissive or subordinate? On the contrary, she looks perky and ready to go!

Fig. 12
A well trained dog!

Figure 13 is what a dog looks like when he's being submissive. He'll instinctively roll on his back, turn away from the fearful stimulus, eyes closed, ears flat against his head, neck and stomach exposed and there may be some involuntary urination. This is not something you can train a dog to

do like you can a 'sit'. "Be submissive" No, it doesn't work like that. A submissive behaviour is innate; it's a natural behaviour; it's part of the dominance/submissive ritualised behaviour.

Fig. 13
A submissive dog – something you cannot teach
Courtesy Jay Lorenz

Pack Rules – The End

If we are going to transpose wolf behaviour to our dogs, which I believe is totally wrong bearing in mind how the domestic dog has diversified so much from the wolf, then let's at least get the wolf behaviour right. The alpha doesn't always eat first; he doesn't always lead the pack; occupy the highest ground; initiate the start of games or attention. In fact all the rules mentioned above are flawed to the point of being ridiculous. They don't apply to wolves and they don't apply to our dogs.

Comparing how wolves behave and then transposing that behaviour into a set of rules as to how we should be treating our dogs, just doesn't work. The dog won't understand what we are trying to do or what message we are trying to convey, so we'll end up with one totally confused dog because we don't have the anatomy or the innate dominant/submissive behaviours to communicate in canine language that the dog will understand.

In its heyday, 'pack rules' were seen as the answer to all behavioural problems, even to some that didn't exist! Some people followed the rules too rigidly and ended up with a fairly miserable dog. Many behaviour counsellors would, and some still do, recommend 'pack rules' to solve a behavioural problem. John Fisher was a canine behaviour counsellor, renowned lecturer, and excellent trainer. He wrote about owners who wanted to be alpha (1997), *"if it's how you want to live with your dog I have news that is going to disappoint a lot of people who have striven to reach this Alpha status – it all means diddly squat to your dog."* This brings me back to the fact that the dog does not perceive itself as part of our 'pack', so all the 'pack rules' are meaningless in terms of canine/human communication.

There is further testament to this fact from McConnell (2002) when she says, *"wolves do a lot of things that we have no reason to emulate, from eating the placenta of their newborn to killing visitors from other packs, so recommending that we humans should do something simply because wolves do is not a compelling argument. Dogs are not behavioural replicates of wolves."*

Given that:

- domestic dogs are not wolves, and neither do they act as if they are

- we can accept that the 'pack rules' are flawed to the point that it's questionable whether they apply to free roaming wolves, let alone dogs

- we can accept that the human family is not a surrogate 'pack' for the dog, but the dog is part of our social unit

then maybe it's time to put an end to applying the outdated, hand-me-down 'pack rules' to our dogs.

Possession Is 9/10ᵗʰ Of The Law

Having accepted a dog for what he is, a domesticated, tame animal, with different behaviours, motivations and emotions than a wolf, we may be in a better position to consider objectively a different, more up-to-date hypothesis of dominance based on science and what we now know about wolf and dog behaviour. Earlier I quoted Overall who says, *"Dominance is a concept found in traditional ethology that pertains to an individual's ability to maintain or regulate access to some resources. It is not to do with status"*. The majority of 'rewards' our dogs can have are basically resources, so 'dominance' is more a question of winning or losing resources, not about gaining a higher status. I also mentioned Resource Holding Potential (RHP) which is the likelihood of an animal engaging in conflict with another, usually of the *same* species, in order to gain or retain a resource. Dogs that have learned that using threats of aggression works in getting, or keeping what they want may develop an expectation of winning conflicts over resources. This has absolutely nothing to do with status and everything to do with the resources the dog values most and the strategies he has developed *through learning* to hang on to them.

This would explain why some dogs might become aggressive if they're turfed off the settee or your favourite chair. It might explain why some dogs guard their food or their toys. If this is the case, then the relationship between dog and owner should be reviewed and changes made at the recommendation of an expert.

Why would a dog become possessive over its toys or your favourite chair?

If left to his own devices, a dog will do whatever he finds emotionally rewarding. If a dog finds that it's rewarding to sleep on the settee and has been allowed to do so for some months, he might take exception to someone suddenly denying him access to that resource and he may start to guard it. Access to the resource has probably gone un-checked or even reinforced for several months, even years. Veterinary neurologist William Klemm (1996) says, *"In ways that are not yet understood, this neural origin of emotions creates internal drives or motivation that guide animals toward goal-*

35

Fig. 14
A comfortable sleeping place – and my chair

directed behaviours." If these 'goal-directed behaviours' are then reinforced, even through non-intervention by the owner, the dog will continue with the behaviour. If the dog then becomes aggressive when the owner tries to remove him from the settee, the owner may misinterpret that aggression as the dog being 'dominant' (that is, trying to raise his status) rather than protecting his resource. In this situation Fisher (1997) writes, *"I'm not convinced they* (dogs) *see life in those terms any more than a spoilt child thinks that he or she is higher ranking than their parents."* Dogs do not understand the concept of ownership but they are aware of resources that are rewarding. Without proper training, the dog is going to get pretty cheesed off if an owner tries to take those resources away.

5. RANK REDUCTION PROGRAMME

When a dog develops a behavioural problem, a common solution has been to impose pack rules but in these cases they are known as a Rank Reduction Programme (RRP). Effectively it means the dog's life is going to be turned upside down and his expected daily rewards will be denied him. According to Fisher and Whitehead (2001), '*If you remove an expected reward, you are in all aspects other than physical, punishing the dog.*' The result of being denied expected rewards and therefore being randomly punished, '*could cause conflict, depression, response suppression, and even helplessness*'. This regime of mental cruelty could suppress the unwanted behaviour, but what happens when life returns to normal? The unwanted behaviour is likely to return.

Given their selection by man to produce behavioural types (and latterly, breeds), quite apart from all the mongrels and crossbreeds, one must also consider if there is ever likely to be any such thing as a standard response dog with predictable behaviour patterns. The emotional relief of frustration at not getting an expected reward can only be gained by either a) increased vigour, and maybe aggression to try and seize the resource, hence problems get worse as the dog tries harder; or b) resignation, that is giving up on expecting to get the reward, hence the dog appears to have changed for the better but has actually become depressed or learned to be helpless.

If we look at these two possibilities of response, think about how you might expect a Labrador to react if you make him sit and wait for food or denied him some other significant reward. How would he feel? How quickly might his restrained frustration evolve into anger, or how long before he might give up waiting and find something else to do? Perhaps quite a while because a Labrador can perhaps endure the frustration better than many breeds. Now think about how a Jack Russell or German Shepherd Dog might react to a similar withholding of food, and your expectation of their endurance of frustration! So how could a 'standard RRP procedure possibly impact on all dogs in the same way in altering their own view of where they fit in the human 'pack', even if it had any effect in the first place? Clearly in each case the individual dog's needs and personality must be assessed. Specific unwanted behaviour must be tackled directly through a specific individual approach to have best chance of success. This comes through teaching and rewarding the dog to behave differently in the problem circumstances, not through a blanket 'cure-all' of a 'rank reduction programme'.

Bear in mind also that selection of dogs by man for breed and type has also impacted on how dogs relate to each other. Two dogs of the same type/breed may have similar values with regard to certain resources, but do Jack Russells, Shelties and Pointers really have the same view of what to do about rats in holes? Think about how this might impact on assessing and treating competitive aggression problems between two dogs sharing a house, such as competition over certain food or access to the owners, both of which can be considered as resources. What effect might it have if both dogs are subjected to a Rank Reduction Programme, or if the owner tries to 'demote' one below the other to create some kind of artificial linear hierarchy?

Do Rank Reduction Programmes Work?

There will always be somebody who has used a 'rank reduction programme' and said it has worked. As John Fisher said, random punishment *suppresses* behaviour and by denying the dog his daily rewards, the dog is being randomly punished. Therefore certain behaviours are suppressed and it may be the behaviour the owners are trying to eradicate is amongst those that are suppressed. But at what cost to the dog psychologically? And what happens when the owners think they've overcome the problem and life returns to normal? Will the unwanted behaviour re-appear? Quite possibly it will, because the **specific** problem has not been addressed.

If we take our settee-loving dog as an example, is he displaying 'dominance' in that he is trying to raise his status? No. Is he guarding a resource? Yes. Therefore there is a singular behavioural 'problem' the owner needs to modify, and it is this **singular problem** that must be addressed directly. A rank reduction programme does **not** treat a singular problem.

I cannot stress enough that if a dog has a behavioural problem, whether it be aggression or just something annoying, the *specific* problem must be addressed. There is no cure-all such as a 'rank reduction programme', so forget pack rules and concentrate on the problem.

A Rank Reduction Programme is a pointless exercise which can psychologically damage the dog. We must remember that dogs are conspecific, in other words *if* they form a pack (and that is something else that is open to question), then they do so with their own species. They won't form a pack in the *true* sense of the word with other species. They won't form a pack with *us*. As they won't form a pack with us what's the point of trying to demote them?

Dogs are social animals and so are we, which is why dogs and people can live together as a social unit; not as a pack, but as a social unit.

6. TIME FOR A RE-THINK

I have purposefully included quotes from people who have actually studied dogs and/or wolves as they support my hypothesis and they put the arguments across much better than I can. All the quotes are related to:

- how different a dog is from a wolf in terms of behaviour and morphology;

- a wolf pack is not run dictatorially but more as a family

- the pack rules we've been told to apply to our dogs are supposedly based on wolf behaviour, which is incorrect as they **don't** apply to wolf behaviour

- the fact that our domestic dogs are trying to gain a higher status over human owners is wrong

- domestic dogs should be treated as domestic dogs and not surrogate wolves.

Just to round off the quotes here are a few more, (and I make no apologies for the number of quotes as long as it gets the point across that we should not be trying to dominate our dogs and they're not part of our pack). Mech (1999) says about a wolf pack, *"In a natural wolf pack, dominance is not manifested as a pecking order and seems to have much less significance than the results of captive packs had implied."* Remember our domestic dog descended from free wolves, not captive ones. Mech also says about the term 'alpha', *"Calling a wolf an alpha is usually no more appropriate than referring to a human parent or roe deer as an alpha. Any parent is dominant to its young offspring, so "alpha" adds no information.....The point here is not so much the terminology but what the terminology **falsely** implies; a rigid, force-based dominance hierarchy."* So Mech, a world authority on free wolves, is also concerned that the term 'alpha' is being misinterpreted.

Dunbar (2006) *"Learning from wolves to interact with pet dogs makes about as much sense as, 'I want to improve my parenting – let's see how the chimps do it!'* This is supported by Coppinger (2001) *"Dogs can't think like wolves because they do not have wolf brains. We descended from apes, but we don't behave like them and we don't think like they do. We are a much different animal than apes in spite of our common ancestry. The same is true of the dog and its ancestor..... I think it is wrong to treat our best friend as a wolf"*

Semyonova (2006) also has concerns about the term 'dominance'. She says, *"The model* (dominance) *has unjustifiably been transferred from its original place in the discussion of the behaviour of wolves to the discussion of the behaviour of dogs....... the phenomenon 'dominance' is questionable, but in any case 'dominance' does not operate as a principle in a social organization of domestic dogs. Dominance hierarchies do not exist and are in fact impossible to construct without entering the realm of human projection and fantasy."*

Steinker (2007) *"Labelling a dog 'dominant' is potentially destructive. Attaching a label to a dog's behaviour or personality can create conflict rather than cohesion in the family".*

Overall (2003) *"Our dogs are dependant on us and they rely on us; we are in a position of guardianship with them."*

While we have been training our dogs to show them we are alpha, putting them through a harsh routine of 'pack rules' that supposedly (but wrongly) reflect wolf behaviour, free wolves continue to live in comparative harmony. Mech (2003) cites biologist Adolph Murie. After a long period of observing free wolves as far back as 1944, he said, *"The strongest impression remaining with me after watching the wolves on numerous occasions was the friendliness."*

When on the move, Peake (personal communication) observed juvenile wolves going back to make sure the older pack members, including a former alpha, were keeping up with the rest of the pack. A wolf pack works co-operatively and they look out for each other. Yet here we are, risking causing physical and/or psychological harm to our dogs because we believe they are members of our 'pack' and we are determined to dominate them and ensure our status as alpha.

With the weight of all the current scientific evidence and what we now know about the differences between wolf and dog behaviour, emotions, motivations, and drives, it is now time to re-think the concept of 'dominance'. Dominance does *not* equate to status between dog and owner, and our domestic dog is *not* trying to raise his status over us. In fact stop thinking about dogs as part of our 'pack'. I can find no evidence to support the 'pack rules' and the owner-must-be-alpha theory. It is now time we confined these 30 year old, out-of-date, hand-me-down theories to history and look at what we know today.

7. WHAT'S TO BE DONE?

How do we get this epitome of obedience if not by dominating the dog? There are now many good training books that explain how to train a dog using positive, motivational methods, and many trainers who use these methods in their class. So find a book and a trainer that does **not** preach 'pack rules' and does **not** train dogs as though they are wolves. There are also many good books explaining how to find and raise a puppy which should have a lot of emphasis on socialisation. Here are a few key points to consider:

- do your homework
- select a good breeder
- socialise the puppy
- teach household etiquette and what the dog is, and is not allowed to do in the home
- start training as early as possible using positive, motivational methods
- be fair to the dog
- be consistent in your training methods and how you treat the dog
- teach the puppy what he is allowed to do indoors and what he's not
- learn to read canine body language and postures.

Do Your Homework

It's very easy to select a breed of dog because of their looks. But looks aren't everything. Find out as much about the breed as you can before you buy one so you have a fair idea of what you're getting and be sure that he will fit in with your lifestyle. If you're not an active family, it's no good getting something like a Border collie or a Springer spaniel. If you don't like the idea of a lot of grooming an Afghan hound would not be a good choice. You wouldn't buy a car or a television just because it looks nice without knowing what you're getting, so don't buy a dog, which is a much more important purchase, without doing your homework.

The Breeder

Always see the dam with her litter when you visit the breeder. Ideally you should find a breeder that raises the litter indoors rather than a kennel in the garden so they can get used to the sights and sounds of household appliances, the hustle and bustle of family life and the comings and goings of different people. The sire should have been carefully selected for his temperament and other attributes the breeder is looking for, and all the hereditary health screening tests have been carried out on both sire and dam. In some cases, CEA or deafness for example, the pups should be tested as well. As the socialisation period starts at a very early age, make sure the breeder has started off the process, so ask what has been done in order to socialise the pup.

Socialisation

The critical period of a puppy's socialisation is roughly between about 4 and 16 weeks. This is the period the puppy will learn that he is a dog and will shape his behaviour when he's an adult. The puppy must be exposed to mild stress so he can cope with life when he's older, meet other dogs, other people and any type of stimuli likely to be faced later on. As the critical period starts at about 4 weeks of age, the breeder has an immense responsibility to start the socialisation process to give the pup a good start in life. This is also the

Fig. 15
Toys for mental stimulation.

Fig. 16
Getting used to Household Appliances.

time to start gentle grooming and inspecting all parts of the puppy's body so he gets used to being handled. However socialisation does not stop at 16 weeks; it's an ongoing process.

House Etiquette

Having got the well-adjusted puppy home, teach him what he is allowed to do in the home and what he is not allowed to do. If you don't want a dog lying on your settee, don't encourage him when he's a puppy. Alternatively, teach a command to invite your puppy onto the sofa so you can have the

company of your dog when you like, but also teach an 'off' command so he will get off when you ask. If you don't want a dog jumping up on people, don't encourage it as a puppy.

Be with the puppy when he is eating; even stroke the puppy, so he becomes comfortable with people being around at meal times. Add a little more food to the bowl while the puppy is eating so he sees a hand by his food bowl as being a good thing.

Fig. 17
Oh well. You can't win them all!

Play games of tug and let the puppy win sometimes. The puppy should perceive games of tug as just that, a game, but don't forget to teach a 'drop' command.

Teach Basic Obedience

It is essential to have a well-mannered dog and very basic training can start when the pup is just a few weeks old. A pups brain grows to 50% of its full size by the time it's just two months old; 80% at four months and fully grown by 12 months (Coppinger, 2001), so training can start very early on in the pup's life. Socialisation and basic obedience go hand-in-hand. Start at home before the pup has completed his inoculations and then by taking your puppy to a training class specifically for puppies so he can learn to interact with puppies of a similar age. Use reward-based, motivational methods of training so the pup finds learning rewarding. The more rewarding, the more he's likely to repeat the behaviour. Include in the training the commands 'drop' and 'leave' which should be taught to a puppy. Unfortunately these commands are usually taught to an adolescent dog when the owner realises how important those commands are when the dog is running around the garden with a pair of the owner's underpants! If you sometimes want your dog to on the sofa with you, teach commands to invite him onto the sofa, and to ask him to get off when you say.

Be Fair

Do not expect the puppy to instantly be the perfect household pet. Teaching house etiquette and basic obedience will take time, so be patient. Dogs can only think and act in canine ways so it will take time for him to learn what we expect of him using our ways of communication. Dogs are happy to live in a social structure. If a structure doesn't exist, the dog will just do whatever it finds rewarding. Do not physically punish your puppy for any wrongdoing. Chances are it was your fault anyway!

Be Consistent

It is very easy to confuse a dog if he is given conflicting commands that are supposed to mean the same thing or he is allowed to do one thing with one member of the family but not another. This may result in the dog developing unwanted behaviours. So be consistent in your commands and how you treat the dog.

Learn to Read Canine Language

We expect dogs to understand our verbal commands and very often a visual cue. It's only right therefore, that we learn to understand what a dog is trying to tell us by learning to 'read' his body posture and facial expression. We will then be in a better position to understand what our dog is trying to tell us; whether he's happy, sad, in pain, needs to be let out to eliminate, at rest or perhaps there may be the onset of a slight problem which could escalate into a major problem if the signs are ignored. A typical example of this is when a dog is left on his own when he's having his meals. If this continues for several months he may become anxious when someone does come into the room when he's eating. A dog that is content to have people in the same room will have his tail in its normal, relaxed position. If there is a slight sway of the tail or it is tucked slightly between his legs, then the pup is showing signs of anxiety and this is the time to take remedial action.

Fig. 18
Relaxed tail position when eating – no problem!

Some dogs will come from a rescue or re-homing centre. Although the principles of what I've said will apply to older dogs, re-homed dogs may already have behavioural problems that will need treatment. They may lack training or they may need special treatment if it's a case of neglect, so older, re-homed dogs must be looked at individually.

7. CONCLUSION

The idea of a dog being 'dominant' originated from observing the behaviour of captive wolf packs. However research by Mech and others shows that a free pack of wolves does not have a dictatorial alpha ruling over the pack. His findings show dominance challenges between wolves are rare, if they exist at all; instead they act as a family, sharing labour. *IF* we were to apply the wolf's behaviour to our dogs, then it's the behaviour from the free packs that we should be looking at and not the observed behaviour of a captive pack that has a more competitive lifestyle.

From the wolf evolved the dog, which has different values to a wolf. Yet the 'pack rules' we are told to use on our dogs are supposed to reflect wolf behaviour. Something doesn't quite fall into place here. To add to the confusion, 'pack rules' are based on canine-to-canine communication but we can only communicate using human methods; we cannot mimic canine behaviour any more than a dog can mimic ours. Dogs are conspecific so they won't perceive themselves as part of our human 'pack', therefore if we try to enforce 'pack rules', the dog won't understand what we are trying to do and we could end up with one very confused, depressed dog.

As we provide all the elements of survival and more for our dog, why would he need to raise his status? Further research by Coppinger on the differences in a dog's predatory motor patterns compared to a wolf's predatory motor patterns, explains more of why our dogs should not be compared to wolves.

Accepting that the dog has evolved from the wolf and is now either a different species or a sub-species (depending on which canine authority you read), we can start to treat him as a dog and not as a wolf in dog's clothing. The dog is not going to be dominant and raise his status in the 'pack' because he's not part of the human 'pack'. Equally, we don't have to be dominant over the dog by using 'pack rules' as they are totally inappropriate and the dog won't understand what we are trying to tell him.

A 'dominant' owner has connotations of aversive or harsh methods to 'teach' or 'train' a dog in order to get their own way. It has connotations of a suppressed dog not being able to truly express his feelings. It has connotations of a lack of bonding and understanding the owner has with their dog.

We have chosen to domesticate the dog and we therefore have a responsibility to understand the dog as best we can. We are both social species which is why we can co-exist together. Dogs have to exist on our terms but we need to be fair, consistent, and be understanding to their needs.

We should have a symbiotic relationship with our dogs; that is, we live together to our mutual benefit. We provide our dog with everything it could possibly need. We in return enjoy the experience of owning a dog because we like dogs; we enjoy their company; we enjoy participating in dog sports and going on long walks with them. If we can accept that our domestic dog does not perceive itself as part of our human 'pack' we can then start to treat a dog for what he actually is – a dog.

Personally, I don't like putting labels on what we think we are in our relationship with our dogs. But if I were to use a label, it would be 'responsible dog owner'; the emphasis on "responsible" and all that goes with it. We don't have to be alpha, dominant or pack leader. All we need to be is an owner responsible for guiding our dog and influencing his behaviour through socialising and training to live in harmony with us and within our society. We also owe it to our dog to learn about dog behaviour so we can understand better our canine companion. If we follow *those* 'rules' we should have no fear of dogs taking over our family.

Wolves Wolves Wolves Wolves . . . . . .

BIBLIOGRAPHY

Abrantes R. (1997) 'The Evolution of Canine Social Behaviour', Wakan Tanka Publishers p. 69, 70

Clutton-Brock J. (1999) 'The Domestic Dog' (ed. Serpell J.) Cambridge University Press p. 9, 15

Coppinger R. & Coppinger L. (2001) 'Dogs. A Startling New Understanding of Canine Origin, Behaviour & Evolution' Scribner, pp 51 – 61, 67, 81, 112, 206, 209, 210

Donaldson J. (1996) 'The Culture Clash', James & Kenneth Publishers, California, p. 19

Dunbar I. (1979) 'Dog Behaviour' t.f.h. Publications p. 84

Dunbar I. (2006) San Francisco Chronicle, October 15, 2006

Fisher J. (1997) 'Diary of a Dotty Dog Doctor' (ed. Whitehead S.) Alpha Publishing, p. 106

Fisher J. and Whitehead S. (2001) 'Advanced Think Dog' course units

Harrington F. and Asa C. (2003) 'Wolves – Behaviour, Ecology, and Conservation' (ed. Mech D. & Boitani L.) University of Chicago Press p.93, 94

Klemm W. (1996) 'Understanding Neuroscience', Mosby-Year Book Inc. p. 198

Kreeger T. (2003) 'Wolves – Behaviour, Ecology, and Conservation' (ed. Mech D. & Boitani L.) University of Chicago Press p. 192, 193

Lindsay S. (2000) 'Handbook of Applied Behaviour and Training Vol. 1' Blackwell Publishing p. 12, 104, 381

Mech. L. D. (1999) 'Alpha, status, dominance, and division of labor in wolf packs' Canadian Journal of Zoology, **77** (8) (1999) p1198, 1200
See: http://fwcb.cfans.umn.edu/courses/fw8576/SocialDynMech_1999.pdf

Mech. L. D. (2000) Leadership in Wolf, *Canis lupus*, Packs. Canadian Field-Naturalist 114(2):259-263. Jamestown, ND: Northern Prairie Wildlife Research Center Online.
See: www.npwrc.usgs.gov/resource/mammals/leader/index.htm

Mech L.D. (2003) 'The Wolf. The Ecology and Behavior of an Endangered Species', University of Minnesota Press, pp. 4, 7, 49, 75, 76, 121, 129, 155, 185

Overall K. (1997) 'Clinical Behavioral Medicine for Small Animals', Mosby-Year Book Inc. pp. 115, 512

Overall K. (2003) US APDT Conference, Orlando

Packard M. (2003) 'Wolves – Behaviour, Ecology, and Conservation' (ed. Mech D. & Boitani L.) University of Chicago Press p.40, 42

Penman S. (1994) 'Veterinary Notes for Dog Owners' (ed. Turner T.) Popular Dogs Publishing p. 489

Pryor K. (2002) 'Don't Shoot the Dog' Ringpress Books, p. 108

Rooney N.J., Bradshaw J.W.S., Robinson I. H. (2000) 'A comparison of dog–dog and dog–human play behaviour', Applied Animal Behaviour Science 66 (2000) 235–248

Semyonova A. (2003) 'The social organization of the domestic dog; a longitudinal study of domestic canine behavior and the ontogeny of domestic canine social systems'. The Carriage House Foundation, The Hague, Netherlands
See: www.nonlineardogs.com (2006 version) p.2, 33

Schmidt P.A. and Mech L.D. (1997) 'Wolf Pack Size and Food Acquisition', American Naturalist 150 (4):513-517. Jamestown ND: Northern Prairie Wildlife Research Center Online.
See: http://www.npwrc.usgs.gov/resource/mammals/wpsize/index.htm

Steinker A. (2007) "Terminology Think Tank: Social dominance theory as it relates to dogs", Journal of Veterinary Behaviour, (2007) 2, 137-140

Zimen E. (1983) 'The Wolf: His Place in the Natural World', Souvenir Press, pp. 26, 27, 30, 173

Wolves Wolves Wolves Wolves . . . .

NOTES

52

NOTES

NOTES